Original title:
Life, Laughter, and Other Strange Questions

Copyright © 2025 Creative Arts Management OÜ
All rights reserved.

Author: Fiona Harrington
ISBN HARDBACK: 978-1-80566-281-5
ISBN PAPERBACK: 978-1-80566-576-2

Whims of Fate

A squirrel stole my snack today,
While I just stood and stared in dismay.
Why do socks disappear in the wash?
Is there a secret sock monster to squash?

The cat plots against me, I swear it's true,
Plotting world domination from the back of the loo.
Why do we trip when we're feeling so spry?
Maybe to show off our balanced reply.

The Unexpected Punchline

Why did the chicken cross the lane?
To get to the hopscotch game, it's plain!
Dogs wagging their tails with grace,
Wonder if they know how they're in the race?

A fish bought a bike, oh what a sight!
Riding around, feeling quite light.
Did you hear about the pie that flew?
It landed in the fruit stand, a perfect brew!

Silliness at the Crossroads

A banana slipped on a peel so sly,
While a turtle waved it goodbye.
Should I wear shoes or float like a breeze?
Oh, decisions are tough when it's snack time, please!

Marshmallows dancing in the quiet night,
Wearing hats made of frosting, what a sight!
What if teapots could sing and twirl?
They'd brew up a storm, oh what a whirl!

Mirages of the Heart

I saw a dream where cucumbers chat,
Discussing the latest hat trends, how about that?
Was there ever a sandwich who dared to fly?
Flying high, just waving goodbye!

The clouds joke with the sun in the sky,
Tickling sunlight as it passes by.
What's the deal with chewed-up pencils?
A secret society of writers' pretzels?

Unearthing the Silly

In a world where ducks wear hats,
And dogs take tea with chatty cats,
We ponder why the sky is blue,
While sneezing bubbles—what a view!

The sun may giggle, clouds may tease,
As penguins waltz among the trees,
Why does the toaster dance at night?
Perhaps it dreams of bread's delight.

Frogs sing opera, toads recite,
With juggling squirrels taking flight,
We search for sense in nonsense schemes,
Embracing quirks, igniting dreams.

So let's unearth the joys untold,
In moments bright, like stars of gold,
For silly sparks, a treasure rare,
Are found in laughter's joyful air.

The Alchemy of Joy

In a cauldron, happiness brews,
With giggles mixed and silly shoes,
A sparkled wand will grant a wish,
To turn plain soup into a dish.

With laughter's dust, we weave the day,
As butterflies join in the play,
We question why the cats can sing,
And wonder if a frog's a king.

The potion bubbles, colors fly,
As dancing pies entice the shy,
If unicorns could tell a joke,
Would they make lemonades from smoke?

From whirling spoons to flying hats,
The joyful chaos surely spats,
We find the warmth in every sigh,
In this alchemy, we learn to fly.

Glee in Disguise

Behind the curtain, shadows prance,
With whimsical hats, they start to dance,
A pickle sings, a snail can skate,
In wobbly shoes, we celebrate.

The clocks may giggle, time will tease,
As jellybeans skip with the breeze,
Questions swirl like cotton candy,
What's so funny? Oh, it's dandy!

A bubble lands upon your nose,
And dances right where laughter flows,
Why do we flip like pancakes grand?
Perhaps it's just a crazy plan!

In every quirk and silly grin,
In glee disguised, we dive right in,
With open hearts and arms held wide,
We'll find the joy that cannot hide.

Dances with the Unexpected

A walrus waltzes, birds all cheer,
As strange surprises draw us near,
With juggling fish and cookie flies,
We chase our joy beneath the skies.

Here comes a shoe that wants to dance,
While cupcakes giggle at their chance,
Around the clock, the minutes twirl,
In joyous chaos, colors swirl.

What if a cactus wore a hat?
Or mice made music with a cat?
The unexpected makes us bold,
With tales of wonder yet untold.

So let's embrace the quirks we find,
With open hearts and curious minds,
For in this beat where laughter plays,
We'll dance through life in silly ways.

Tides of Amusement

In a world of silly hats,
The penguins dance at dawn.
With pancakes on their tails,
They waddle and then yawn.

Giggles float like bubbles,
In a pool of jelly beans.
A cat that plays the trumpet,
Is where the humor gleans.

Every fork held backward,
Is a spatula in disguise.
Banana peels in pathways,
Bring forth unexpected cries.

So gather 'round the circus,
Where giggles chase the stars.
With juggles and with chuckles,
We'll laugh until it's ours.

The Joyful Enigma

In a puzzling riddle box,
A hamster spins in glee.
With socks upon its ears,
It dances, can't you see?

What's the secret to the laughter?
Is it tickles or a tease?
A rubber chicken on a throne,
Can bring us all to knees.

In the mirror, faces switch,
A crab is wearing shoes.
With every twist and tangle,
The mystery just ensues.

So let's twirl in question marks,
With grins that stretch so wide.
For joy is found in oddity,
Let it be our guide.

When Ordinary Becomes Extraordinary

When Tuesday turned to giggle,
And socks began to sing,
The ordinary chair became,
A throne for everything.

Spaghetti on a Tuesday night,
Turned into a disco feast.
With meatballs doing the cha-cha,
The laughter never ceased.

A teapot that tells stories,
By whistling through the years,
Turns mundane chats to crazy tales,
And fills our hearts with cheers.

In a world of borrowed whims,
The plain wears fancy shoes.
Let's toast to those odd moments,
Where the strange becomes our muse.

Celebrating the Curious Spirit

With a twist of lime and laughter,
The ants host a grand parade.
Marching under a rainbow,
With cheerleading frogs displayed.

The clouds wear polka dots,
As the sun does a silly jig.
When questions get a punchline,
Curiosity gets big!

A sock hops down the sidewalk,
With a story yet untold.
Its wacky wanderings guide us,
To adventures brave and bold.

So let's dance with odd ideas,
And tip our hats to night.
For in this playful wonder,
Every whim is pure delight.

Quirks of the Human Condition

In the morning, mismatched socks,
A dance with coffee, joy in flocks.
Mirror winks at the untidy hair,
Countless oddities fill the air.

Chasing pigeons in the park,
They scatter like a sudden spark.
Tickling grass beneath our feet,
Every moment's a playful treat.

Whispers of secrets in the breeze,
Giggles as we stumble with ease.
A world that spins on a crooked axis,
Each twist and turn, a funny praxis.

In the end, it's all a show,
A jester's grin, a cosmic glow.
So let's embrace each silly quirk,
And dance among the human work.

Mirthful Meditations

In a bubble bath with rubber ducks,
Floating dreams and giggling lucks.
A bathtub concert, splashes high,
Singing softly to the sky.

Beneath the stars, we juggle thoughts,
Imaginary friends in all their spots.
Talking trees and laughter's echo,
Whimsical tales in moonlit meadow.

Dancing shadows on the wall,
Each step a giggle, each twirl, a fall.
Our careless hearts, so free to spree,
In this bizarre comedy.

With every reach for blissful grace,
We stumble often, but find our place.
In simple joys, we learn to see,
The art of fun in absurdity.

Inside the Laughter Vault

Peeking inside where shadows play,
A treasure chest of jesters' sway.
With every chuckle that we make,
The sun shines brighter, great heartache.

Jokes are love notes tied with string,
Each twist and turn a playful fling.
Crafted tales of every day,
Unsung heroes, all at play.

Bananas slip and pigeons dance,
Who knew life was a silly chance?
Sprinkled joy in a world so bleak,
We find our giggles when we're weak.

So dive deep within this stash,
Let laughter burst forth, not in a flash.
For in this vault, we all belong,
A symphony of joy in a quirky song.

The Puzzles We Create

A riddle wrapped in silly hats,
Why do we question where laughter sat?
With every twist comes a mystery,
The answer hides in our history.

Grinning cats and talking dogs,
Wiggling worms in muddy bogs.
Every problem, a clue left behind,
In the laughter, delight we find.

Frog leaps high, skipping stones,
A fantastical world in quirky tones.
Upside down, we ponder, grin,
The puzzles of joy that dwell within.

So let's frolic through this maze,
With childlike wonder, we'll amaze.
For in these quirks and funny signs,
We seek the joy that brightly shines.

The Playful Paradox

In a world where socks tend to mismatch,
Cats chase their tails with fervent dispatch.
Bananas wear hats, or so they pretend,
Jokes tumble forth, around every bend.

A spoon tells a fork, 'You're such a fine friend!'
While the table takes bets on the dog's latest trend.
Life's a big circus, full of strange sights,
With elephants tap dancing on frosty nights.

Dreamscapes and Delights

A moonbeam slipped into my shoe,
While jellybeans rapped a soft tune.
I danced with a dragon, who played the flute,
He wore a bright hat with a shiny old boot.

A cloud shaped like pizza drifted on by,
Filled with toppings that twinkled like stars in the sky.
Oh, the dreams that unfold when the day is done,
Where clouds serve up laughter and every joke's fun!

Vignettes of the Unexpected

A penguin in slippers walks into a café,
Orders a latte and shuffles away.
Goldfish in bow ties cheer him with glee,
As a parrot posts selfies on social decree.

A rooster in shades sings blues by the pool,
While turtles compete in a game of cool.
Each moment a snapshot, bizarre yet divine,
In the gallery of odd, we're all in line.

Behind the Curtain of Delight

Behind the curtain, a rabbit takes flight,
With carrots as wings, in the gentle twilight.
A wizard with giggles turns water to wine,
As fish flaunt their fins, dressed up and divine.

A whispering breeze sneaks in with a tune,
Tickling the daisies, a merry monsoon.
The world's a grand stage, quirky and bright,
Where the odd ends of joy dance into the night.

Sprinkles of Serendipity

On Tuesday, shoes go mismatched,
Cookies dance when they're batch-matched.
An umbrella flops in the breeze,
Laughter hides in the silliest Keys.

Bananas peel in a grand ballet,
While cats in hats ask if they can play.
The toaster whispers, 'Let's make toast!'
And crumbs turn into a curious ghost.

Sidewalks chuckle under the moon,
As jellybeans sing a silly tune.
Time slips by on roller skates,
As we ponder about garden gates.

Show me a sock that's lost its match,
In this crazy world, that's quite the catch.
Every twist and turn, a jolly jest,
In the silly soup, we're truly blessed.

Questions on the Wind

Why do clouds wander up so high?
Do shoes on the line ever try to fly?
When does a pinecone decide to dance,
While everybody else just takes a chance?

Is it true that frogs wear tiny crowns?
Do they giggle when no one's around?
Can a tumbleweed really get lost,
In the search for the friend it'll cost?

What happens when music turns to cheese?
Do singing mice find it hard to squeeze?
Does the moon play hide and seek at night,
With stars that twinkle just out of sight?

What if dreams could sew a new coat?
Wouldn't that be a funny little note?
As questions twirl like leaves in spring,
The winds remind us of everything!

The Jester's Reflection

In the mirror, a jester grins wide,
With mismatched socks, he can't hide.
His hat's a circus, spinning in tune,
While he juggles thoughts from morning till noon.

Did you hear about the fish that sings?
He's off to court with a couple of flings.
Each bubble pops with a giggling sound,
Creating ripples of joy all around.

What if apples started to dance?
Would they join carrots in a leafy romance?
And should we clap when cucumbers croon,
In the grand performance of afternoon?

With every chuckle, a riddle unfolds,
As the jester, with grace, shares tales untold.
In his kingdom of winks and silly quests,
He reigns supreme, for he knows best!

Anatomy of a Smile

A smile is made of giggles and cheer,
Sprinkled with kindness, oh so dear.
It dances on lips, a mysterious art,
Creating a spark in every heart.

Add a dash of joy and a pinch of mirth,
Whipped up with dreams, and it's full of worth.
Let's mix in some laughter, loud and bright,
And watch it glow in the soft moonlight.

What's the secret? A wink or two,
Maybe it's all about sharing a view.
With candy-coated eyes, we find our way,
Turning the ordinary into a play.

Frowns may visit, but they never stay,
For smiles spin tales that chase clouds away.
In this anatomy of joy, we all take part,
With every chuckle, we mend the heart.

Souls in Search of Smiles

Through alleys where giggles collide,
Mismatched socks dance with pride.
A cat in a hat, oh what a sight,
Chasing shadows into the night.

Flowers wear boots, how absurd!
They gossip and gossip without a word.
Crickets play tunes on a tiny stage,
While ants discuss tales of the age.

In fields where thoughts do leap and twirl,
Butterflies debate, they spin and swirl.
All's fair in the games they play,
With giggles drifting far away.

Oh, for a tickle from the breeze,
To bounce with the trees at their knees.
In this dance, let souls unwind,
Seeking the smiles that they can find.

An Inquiry Into the Absurd

Why do shoes prefer to hide?
In bushes where oddities abide?
Does a matchstick crave to ignite?
In the middle of an empty night?

Whispers from old chairs, they croon,
While teapots simmer a merry tune.
Chickens gather for a debate,
On how to cross the road and wait!

Noses wrinkle at questions so deep,
Like why do socks go missing in sleep?
With every twirl, the answers bend,
Yet giggles sprinkle, that's the trend.

To ponder these quirks is quite a feat,
In a world that spins with funny feet.
Join in the fun, let thoughts collide,
For the absurd is where dreams reside.

The Color of Curiosity

What if clouds wore polka dots?
And rain danced on giant pots?
Each drop a secret, bright and bold,
In hues of laughter, tales unfold.

Trees wear spectacles, how they see!
As squirrels ponder the world's decree.
With each squirrely twist and turn,
The colors of wonder brightly burn.

Fish in bow ties swim with flair,
While hawks debate floating in air.
What stories do puddles tell,
Of mirthful moments and wishes that swell?

So let's paint with questions, bright and grand,
In a canvas where smiles expand.
For each curious thought, a laugh drops in,
Creating a world where joy begins.

Threads of Joyful Inquiry

What if spaghetti could speak French?
At dinner tables, they'd start a wrench.
Macaroni in coats, oh what a show!
Debating their fate with a sauce below.

Jellybeans, oh, what a treat!
Café conversations so very sweet.
With flavors that giggle under the sun,
They wonder if candy could ever run.

Questions unravel like yarn in the breeze,
As kittens chase after thoughts with ease.
Pockets filled with dreams and more,
They search for happiness in each door.

So let's weave our threads in radiant hues,
Of laughter, of wonders, of curious views.
For every inquiry, a smile's disguise,
In this tapestry where joy never dies.

Riddles in the Sunlight

Bubbles pop in the air, so bright,
Chasing shadows, a curious sight.
Tickles dance on a breeze, full of cheer,
What's the answer? It's funny, I fear.

Jesters jump in a field of gold,
Every giggle a story waiting to be told.
Clocks spin backward, the grass sings loud,
An invisible audience, a bustling crowd.

Pies in windows, a tempting charade,
Who gets the last slice? It's all a trade.
Sunset whispers riddles in a swirl,
Chasing the moonlight, a dizzying twirl.

Sunflowers laugh, their faces aglow,
As butterflies dance in a whimsical show.
In this world of jest and silly roams,
We gather moments, like brightly blown foam.

Tangles of Time and Tickles

Twisted dreams on a swirl of air,
Clocks with legs, they run everywhere.
A tickle of thought, a chuckle from skies,
What if time was a jester in disguise?

Noses painted red in playful glee,
Running in circles, just you and me.
Every question's a merry-go-round,
In spaces where silly wisdom abounds.

Whimsical paths in kaleidoscope views,
Stepping on clouds, wearing mismatched shoes.
Finding a penny could mean a great fate,
As we wonder, why did we wait?

Backwards our steps, yet forward we fly,
Chasing our tails and the sun kissed pie.
Every second a giggle, every laugh a rhyme,
In the tangle of stories that play with time.

The Enigmatic Dance of Being

In the center of chaos, a dance unfolds,
Jellybeans spinning, their laughter bold.
Each step a question, each twirl a tease,
What do you get when you jiggle knees?

Bananas talking in perky tones,
While octopuses juggle their sparkling cones.
What's the secret? A wink or a grin,
As the rhythm of whims makes the world spin.

Roosters in tutus, striking poses bright,
Chasing the shadows, oh what a sight!
In this puzzling ball where nothing's quite right,
We giggle and scamper into the night.

Puzzles of laughter, wrapped tight with string,
Tickles of joy that the odd moments bring.
If being is teasing, then let it be fun,
We'll dance through the riddles until we've spun.

Giggles Beneath the Surface

Under the waves, where creatures play,
Bubbles burst forth, giggling all day.
What swims with glee in a deep ocean blue?
A fish with a mustache, just passing through.

Mirthful squids paint with witty flair,
While starfish snicker, they don't have a care.
Each ripple of laughter, a splash of surprise,
In waters of jest, where the strange swims and flies.

Clownfish in costumes, dappled and bright,
Join the parade in the shimmering light.
Questions float by on bubbles of air,
What truly matters? We don't need to care.

Delightfully tangled in glee and in mirth,
Finding our joy from the depths of the earth.
Under the surface, where laughter reflects,
We ponder the wonders, and just can't object.

Whispers of the Everyday

In a town where socks play hide and seek,
A cat steals the spotlight, so unique.
Bananas slip on their yellow shoes,
While the dog dreams of chasing the moon's views.

A toaster sings tunes at the break of dawn,
While coffee beans dance, sleepy but drawn.
The clock ticks slowly, then races ahead,
As daydreams of pancakes float out of bed.

Each pebble holds tales of the stroll we take,
And ducks in the pond make a splash for fun's sake.
With giggles echoing under the sun's ray,
The world spins in quirks, come what may.

A tale of a spoon that wished to be fork,
And a fridge that hums a familiar quirk.
These whispers of whimsy weave through our day,
In the oddest of moments, our hearts find their way.

The Curious Chronicles

Once a shoe claimed it could pirouette,
While a teacup witnessed dance parties, you bet!
The cats on the fence held a council of night,
Debating the merits of shadows and light.

In gardens, the flowers share gossip so bright,
With daisies remarking on bees taking flight.
A squirrel in sunglasses monitors all,
Making notes about how to catch winter's fall.

The sun wears a hat, quite dapper and bold,
While raindrops tell stories as they drip and unfold.
With curious twists, the mysteries grow,
As each moment unfolds, it's a glorious show.

In a land where the odd and the strange intertwine,
Every heartbeat a riddle, each laugh a sign.
The chronicles written in colors so grand,
We venture together, hand in hand.

Echoes of Joyful Misfits

Picture a penguin in a top hat so fine,
Twirling on ice, a dazzling design.
Pigs in the air, with wings all aglow,
And mice in tuxedos putting on a show.

A talking tree shares secrets of old,
While the clouds play chess on a board made of gold.
With whispers of laughter dancing on breeze,
The misfits unite with the greatest of ease.

Balloons float by, holding dreams in their grasp,
While fish in the sea wear their finest clasp.
Together they giggle at the oddity's game,
As the world spins round, nothing stays the same.

In patches of joy, where the wacky reside,
A spark of connection in the strange we confide.
Echoes ring out, a fabulous tale,
Of misfits embracing, together they sail.

Musings of a Wandering Heart

A shoe on the path speaks tales of the weary,
With road signs giving advice just a bit eerie.
Clouds play tag with the sun in the blue,
While stardust drips down, wrapping us too.

A bicycle dreams of adventures afar,
While the streetlamp wiggles like a shy star.
With each twist and turn, stories unfold,
In places most curious, daring and bold.

A wandering pen scribbles thoughts in the air,
Chasing the giggles of ghosts without care.
With each bubbling laugh, we wander anew,
Through gardens of whimsy, a magical view.

In the wonder we search, hearts skip and dart,
Painting our journeys with splashes of art.
For in every question, strange and refined,
A tapestry woven uniquely aligned.

The Humor of Life's Mysteries

In the garden of oddities, blooms a delight,
Tickling the thoughts like a feathered flight.
Why did the chicken cross roads with a grin?
To show all the traffic just what could've been.

A cat wearing glasses reads on the floor,
Sipping its tea while it ponders the score.
What's at the end of a rainbow's parade?
Just socks with the secrets they long to evade.

The toaster is judging, oh what a sight,
While spoons protest loudly, 'We deserve more light!'
What's funny in silence, a giggle set free?
When mirrors respond with a wink, just for me.

In Quest of the Unusual

A monkey in pajamas did dance on a hill,
Debating with shadows, they giggle and thrill.
What fuels the merry, the giddy delight?
Perhaps it's the nonsense that twinkles at night.

A clown with a briefcase walks into a bar,
Looking for punchlines that drift like a star.
Is humor a treasure buried under the ground?
Or merely a wisp of the silly profound?

The fish in the bowl wears a tiny top hat,
Claiming it's royalty, bold, where it's at.
What's strangeness, we ask, if it's dressed up in gold?
With stories that shimmer, eternally told.

A Journal of Curious Delights

An octopus scribbles poems on a shell,
With ink made of squirt, casting quite a spell.
Why do socks vanish in the depths of the wash?
Because they found a party, all snug in a posh.

A turtle recites jokes under a tree,
While ants form a band, as busy as can be.
What's the secret of laughter that bubbles inside?
It's tickling the fancies we never can hide.

A shoe with a mustache struts down the lane,
Proclaiming it's destined to dance in the rain.
In curious tomes, we scribble and jot,
For every odd moment is a memory caught.

Echoes of the Unseen

In the attic, a ghost plays the drums with delight,
While shadows conspire to dance through the night.
What whispers of giggles hide underneath beds?
The tales of the foolish, the dreams of the heads.

A pineapple recites lines, so bold and absurd,
Claiming its wisdom is lost in the word.
Could cookies be judges in a court of the sweet?
As cakes weigh the options of frosting to meet.

The chimes of the clock laugh and tickle the air,
Riddles unspoken, yet oh, so aware.
What's fanciful chaos if not pure delight?
A carnival moving through shadows and light.

The Symphony of the Unseen

In quiet corners, echoes play,
Bouncing off the walls of day.
A giggle in the breeze does sway,
Invisible notes that drift away.

The clock strikes odd, the chimes are wild,
A hidden tune, a playful child.
With every step, the ground is smiled,
Odd notes in harmony compiled.

In shadows dance the whispers bright,
With twist and twirl, they take to flight.
Crafting rhythms in the night,
A silly waltz, a comical sight.

So join the dance of skewed delight,
Where nonsense reigns and dreams take flight.
Just listen close, embrace the light,
For laughter hides in wondrous height.

Beneath the Surface of Cheer

Underneath a sunny grin,
A gopher pokes his tiny chin.
He chuckles softly, tucked in thin,
While squirrels plot their cheeky sin.

Around the bend, a turtle hums,
To the beat of drumming crumbs.
A party starts, with joyful plums—
A feast of jokes that never comes.

The daisies wink with secret puns,
While butterflies make silly runs.
In hidden nooks, the laughter stuns,
As bubbles burst like frothy guns.

So dive beneath this jolly trap,
Where giggles swim and stories flap.
Count how many in the cap,
A treasure trove, a thoughtless map.

Reflections of an Open Mind

In mirrors held at oddest angles,
Ideas twist like fables dangles.
Thoughts collide, the laughter wrangles,
As reason hides and chaos tangles.

The cat's awake, with eyes aglow,
It ponders truths we may not know.
A ponder pout, a slightly low,
Still catches quirks with gentle flow.

We march in rows of mismatched shoes,
Spilling thoughts like vibrant hues.
Between the lines, the nonsense brews,
And every glance gives us our cues.

So take a glimpse inside this maze,
Where giggles dance in curious ways.
And in the twinkling, we'll amaze,
The comic hearts in gentle rays.

Jests Between the Lines

Each page a riddle, filled with jest,
A plot that teases, weaves the best.
With hidden quirks, it leaves us pressed,
In laughter's arms, we're all at rest.

The author grins from outside time,
Crafting mismatched thoughts that rhyme.
Every twist is quite sublime,
An echo wraps in playful chime.

Characters leap, in leaps of faith,
Through silly mess, they dance with wraith.
Their secret smiles, a lovely wraith,
Composing joy, a lively swathe.

So turn the page and let it spin,
Where jests abound and smiles begin.
In every corner, joy's a twin,
A merry heart will always win.

Jokes Written in the Wind

A feather danced and then it swayed,
It whispered secrets, mischief played.
With gusts that tickled every ear,
The world erupted into cheer.

Clouds chuckled softly, what a sight,
As shadows wiggled, taking flight.
The sun joined in with a silly grin,
A breeze of giggles from within.

Trees formed jokes in rustling leaves,
As squirrels plotted to deceive.
They'd leap and skip, a grand ballet,
While nature laughed and danced away.

And in this jest of sun and air,
Each moment fizzled with a flare.
So chase the wind that laughs and leaps,
For humor's found where nature keeps.

The Joy of Misplaced Socks

Oh, where have all my socks now gone?
One's off to dance at the break of dawn.
The other's playing hide-and-seek,
With mystery lurking behind the creek.

A lone sock sits upon the chair,
As if it's plotting, unaware.
"Join me for the missing sock ball!"
It shouts aloud, "Let's have a ball!"

Behind the dryer, a party's held,
With mismatched pairs, all are compelled.
They snicker and wiggle in delight,
While I am stuck with one sock in sight.

So here's to those who wander wide,
And to the socks that will not bide.
In every hole and nook they trot,
A humorous chase for each lost lot.

Wonders over Morning Coffee

A cup of warmth, the morning's kick,
With swirling dreams, the clock goes tick.
Each sip is filled with playful grace,
As thoughts do dance and dreams embrace.

I ponder why my toast is burnt,
While chucking butter, dreams are churned.
A sprinkle of sugar, a dash of fun,
In this caffeinated race I run.

The spoon performs a tiny jig,
A whisk that sings, both sharp and big.
Each creak of chairs, a laugh or two,
In this café of whims, all feels new.

So let the day pour in with cheer,
As coffee brews, our smiles appear.
For wonder's found in every brew,
With each giggle and laugh anew.

The Humor of the Ordinary

In sidewalks cracked and worn with age,
Each step's a joke upon the stage.
The pigeons coo with such finesse,
While people trip without duress.

A bicycle wobbles, speed unwound,
As laughter echoes all around.
A dog that chases his own tail,
Brings smiles and joy without fail.

The morning rush, a comic show,
With coffee spills and overflow.
The bus arrives late, what a sight,
We'll toast to chaos, pure delight!

So raise a glass to all who roam,
For in the ordinary, we find home.
With chuckles shared and stories spun,
The humor's here for everyone.

Reveries of a Curious Mind

In the corner, a sock went astray,
Yearning for freedom, it danced all day.
A cat on the window, plotting a leap,
While pondering secrets the goldfish keep.

Why does the moon wear such a smug grin?
Is it hiding a joke that it knows from within?
The toaster chuckles at the bread's fate,
As it pops up and dances, feeling first-rate.

When a shoe starts to squeak, does it sing?
Whispers of friendship between each spring?
A pancake debates if it's round or square,
An existential crisis, and who will care?

With each little question, a giggle appears,
Chasing the shadows and shedding our fears.
The curious heart finds the world quite absurd,
In the fun of the moment, we never prefer.

Syllables of Surprise

A frog tried to leap but tangled its tongue,
In his leap of ambition, oh how he had sprung!
He questioned his choices with every small croak,
Did he leap for a lily or a giant oak?

A cactus sent postcards from the dune,
Wishing to dance in the light of the moon.
But prickly and proud, it just sat with a sigh,
Dreaming of twirls under the starry sky.

The sandwich was startled when it got a call,
From a pickle, quite eager to join in the ball.
"Let's relish the moment," it said with a cheer,
And they pictured a banquet that called them near.

With each quirky thought, the world spins around,
Joys in the oddities waiting to be found.
Who knew that a laugh could bloom in your chest,
In syllables sprung from a heart so impressed?

Laughter in the Margins

In the margins of pages, a doodle would dance,
With a smile so wide, full of whimsy and prance.
A snail in a top hat and monocle, too,
Taunting the ants to indulge in the view.

The corners of books hold secrets so sly,
Like a turtle's slow race to the sweet pie in the sky.
Whispers of laughs on a breeze through the trees,
Make the oddities laugh, if you please.

Once a butterfly sat on a muffin so bright,
Posing for pictures, what a charming sight!
While crumbs in the air formed a confetti parade,
For a party of dreams that would never fade.

In every odd moment, a chuckle awaits,
With hilarity softening the hardest of fates.
Ink stains and giggles paint life on the edge,
Where laughter is found, we can always pledge.

Fragments of Joy

A spoon was convinced it could dance like a king,
To the rhythm of oatmeal, it started to sing.
While forks rolled their eyes, feeling jealous and mad,
Jumping on plates, they deemed it quite bad.

A dog and a fish shared a giggly chat,
On the nature of crunchy versus being fat.
"Oh, the thrill of the chase and the hunt for a snack,
Let's plot an adventure, but watch for the cat!"

Clouds wearing mustaches drifted on by,
Their puffs of white cotton all twinkled with sighs.
They whispered to grasses what fun it could be,
If only they could laugh just like you and me.

In fragments of oddness, true merriment springs,
We juggle our questions like circus-like kings.
Find the joy in the quirky, the silly, the true,
In every strange thought, there's a spark waiting for you.

Chuckles in the Moonlight

In the stillness where shadows creep,
A cat with a bowtie makes meep.
The stars giggle as they twinkle bright,
While frogs in tuxedos dance with delight.

A sandwich sings a tune so sweet,
As pickles and mustard take a seat.
Moonbeams tickle the roots of a tree,
And I wonder, who serves the tea?

A cowboy rides a roller skate,
Chasing a chicken who knows her fate.
Whispers of giggles float through the night,
As dreams pack their bags for morning flight.

And though the world may seem quite absurd,
A wink from the moon says, "Have you heard?"
In this realm of jests and silly sights,
The heart finds joy in the moonlit nights.

Tales from the Offbeat Path

Upon a path where oddities bloom,
A cactus in slippers whispers, "Room!"
With boots made of marshmallows so soft,
Clouds play hopscotch, floating aloft.

A squirrel with glasses reads a book,
While a pudding cup sings with a shook.
Kites made of pasta dance in the breeze,
And we laugh as the beetles tease.

Jellybeans gather for a round of poker,
While hula-hooping turtles grow bolder.
The sun throws confetti, oh what a show,
As giggles and grins begin to grow.

Every twist and turn brings us delight,
In a world that swirls like a kite in flight.
So follow the path where the strange things lay,
And let happiness guide you on the way.

Wonder and Whimsy

In a realm where questions pair and dance,
A pancake offers to take a chance.
With syrupy wisdom, it tells me please,
To flip for the answers in the breeze.

A pair of socks form a rock band,
Pumping rhythms that make you stand.
Bananas wearing shades strut with flair,
Spreading cheer like they just don't care.

Cupcakes debate on their frosting type,
While sprinkles compete for a shining hype.
The moon cracks a joke, the stars burst out,
And giggles erupt all about.

So grab your sense of whimsy and roam,
In a world that feels like a sweetened poem.
Dance with the silly, sing with delight,
And let your imagination take flight.

A Serendipitous Journey

On a journey where hiccups lead the way,
A snail with a backpack shouts, "Hooray!"
With each tiny step, a story unfolds,
Of marshmallow castles and unicorn gold.

With butterflies wearing top hats in tow,
They share secrets only they seem to know.
Lemons in limos roll down the lane,
Chasing laughter while dancing in rain.

A llama with dreams of high fashion,
Struts 'round the corner with stylish passion.
While giggling geese honk out a rhyme,
The world spins on in a comical time.

So take a leap into the bizarre,
Where strange is the norm, and joy's not far.
In this merry land of surprises so true,
Each step feels like magic, just waiting for you.

The Hidden Harmony

In the garden of dreams, where giggles bloom,
A cat dances by, swiping dust with a broom.
A squirrel in a suit, so dapper and spry,
Juggles acorns as clouds drift lazily by.

Whispers of shadows, the mink in the hat,
Tells tales of the moon, and the sun's silly chat.
With a twinkle in eye, and a pineapple grin,
The orchestra plays, let the chaos begin!

Roosters that stumble, in shoes made of cheese,
Chasing round rabbits, who giggle with ease.
They paint the sky purple, with laughter so bright,
Creating a rainbow in the dead of the night.

So let's twirl on the grass, with marshmallows crowned,
For joy's in the laughter, where silliness found.
In this hidden harmony, a party bizarre,
We dance with the stars, getting lost in the czar.

Chronicle of the Ticklish Soul

Once upon a day, in a land filled with cheese,
A ticklish soul giggled beneath shaking trees.
With socks made of jelly, and shoes lined with fluff,
Each step was a bounce, oh, that tickly stuff!

The moon played the fiddle, while the stars made a pie,
And frogs in bowties agreed to comply.
A waltz of wafting whispers floated on air,
As laughter echoed, without any care.

Then came a parade of bright polka-dots,
With chattering teapots, and laughter-like knots.
They danced on a tightrope, of sweet candy cane,
With grins that could brighten the cloudiest rain.

Oh, the ticklish soul with a riddle in sight,
Asks if jellybeans come from the stars at night.
With mischief abounding, let wisdom unwind,
In this chronicle's heart, pure chaos defined.

Moments that Make Us Wonder

A pickle in a top hat, prancing with flair,
Questions the rainbows, and fragrances rare.
In corners of laughter, a puzzle unfolds,
With giggles of kittens, their antics retold.

Above, the clouds are made of cotton candy,
While stuck-up umbrellas refuse to be handy.
The clocks seem to giggle, and tickle the sun,
Would time ever pause in this frolicsome fun?

An octopus, juggling, in a sea made of cream,
Speaks of odd wonders, like a whacky daydream.
What's magic, what's mischief, beneath the sand's sway?
Moments that dazzle, slip softly away.

So cherish the odd, and those quirky delights,
For giggles and gaffes are the best kind of sights.
In the dance of the silly, let curiosity wend,
As we ponder the laughs, and the joys they send.

Embracing the Slightly Irregular

In the land of the slightly, the whimsical roam,
Where bananas wear goggles, and turtles build homes.
Blue penguins in bowties, go off on a spree,
Serenading the daisies with sweet symphony.

The teapot is grumpy, it starts to complain,
While socks have debates on who's winning the game.
A llama with sunglasses, struts down the lane,
With a wink and a nudge, in odd, silly rain.

Here's to missing buttons and shoes that don't match,
To the dance of the inexplicable as we catch.
Each chuckle a treasure, a glimpse of the bright,
In the embrace of the quirky, we twirl with delight.

So let's toast to the odd with a giggle and cheer,
For life's little questions grow sweeter each year.
In the realm of the funny, we learn and we play,
As we dance through the moments, come join in the fray!

A Mosaic of Mirth

In the garden of giggles, we play,
Chasing shadows that dance and sway.
A squirrel steals snacks from a picnic scene,
While we chuckle at what might have been.

Jellybeans rain from a sky of blue,
Surprising the folks who don't have a clue.
A cat wears a hat, it's quite the sight,
As feathers float gently, drifting light.

Unicorns prance on marshmallow clouds,
While the sun beams brightly amidst the crowds.
Tickles and teasing, a joyous mix,
In a world where reality rarely sticks.

Worms in tuxedos tap dance with glee,
To the tune of a frog playing the key.
Here's to the moments we cannot explain,
We laugh at the chaos, it's all in the game.

The Art of Questioning

Why do pancakes fly when you're in a rush?
And why do kites wheeze out a whoosh?
Do socks ever wonder where their mates go,
As they tumble and twirl in a laundry show?

Whispers of jellyfish ask why they glow,
As curious ants march in a straight row.
Did you see the llama with rollerblade wheels?
Or the plant that sings all of its meals?

When does a toaster have its day off,
Or does it live free while the oven just scoffs?
Is the moon really cheese, or what do we think?
And is the sun just a giant donut in pink?

Let us ponder the wonders far and wide,
With silly ideas as our joyful guide.
For in every question, a giggle is stored,
Leading us onward where laughter is poured.

Chronicles of a Jolly Heart

In the land of chatter where giggles bloom,
A crab wears a crown, claiming his room.
He dances in circles, a regal display,
While seagulls roll dice as they eat their prey.

The clock ticks in riddles, it chimes with cheer,
As donuts jog past, munching on beer.
With a wink and a nudge, the world goes round,
Dragons play hopscotch on whimsical ground.

Every raindrop that falls bursts into song,
Painting the sky with colors so strong.
A rainbow parades, waving hands in the air,
To the tune of a cat doing a butt-shake affair.

Chirpy companions gather near the pond,
Sprinkling giggles with every fond.
For a jolly heart finds joy in small bits,
Creating a history of playful wit.

Mischief in the Mundane

Socks conspire over cups of tea,
Planning their adventure to the wildest spree.
A broom sings softly to the moon at night,
While the fridge tells jokes, delightfully slight.

Paperclips giggle in a stack on the desk,
As the stapler sneezes, making quite the mess.
Who knew kitchen pots were such gossip queens?
Sharing the secrets of our daily routines.

An old shoe tells stories of journeys afar,
While the toothpaste tries hard to be a star.
Each shelf is alive with whispers and sighs,
A world full of wonders beneath our own eyes.

Mundane turns magical with a sprinkle of fun,
As our everyday things leap and run.
For in each corner, mischief does spark,
Turning the ordinary into a whimsical lark.

Explorations in Euphoria

In a world where cats wear hats,
And the moon winks at silly chats,
We dance on clouds made of fluff,
Laughing at all the strange stuff.

Jellybeans rain from the sky,
Pigs in tuxedos fly high,
Tickles take flight on a breeze,
As we chase after squeaky cheese.

Worms with glasses read the news,
Bouncing around in their bright shoes,
They giggle and tell tales untold,
Of adventures in lands of gold.

So take a step on this wild ride,
Embrace the quirks that so abide,
With giggles loud and spirits free,
Explore this joy with glee and glee.

Whispers of the Everyday

Socks that dance without a pair,
Teacups chat without a care,
The toaster pops with words to say,
A quirk in every mundane day.

Umbrellas that open just for fun,
They twirl in circles, on the run,
Raindrops wear their party hats,
As we tiptoe among the chitchats.

Birds recite the jokes they heard,
Chirping tales of the absurd,
Butterflies laugh in faint allure,
While ants debate a game of lure.

In corners where shadows play,
Life's oddities have their say,
With smiles sparkling here and there,
Whispers of whimsy fill the air.

Giggles in the Quiet

In stillness where absurdities hum,
Tickles echo, a gentle drum,
Silly thoughts that jive and sway,
While seriousness drifts away.

A chair that squeaks a secret tune,
The clock giggles through the afternoon,
Lampshades nod with a knowing glance,
As shadows leap to join the dance.

Cacti wear their prickly crowns,
Chuckling at the world in frowns,
Bananas slide in a playful race,
Inviting smiles to every face.

In quiet corners, jokes lay still,
Ready to spark a sudden thrill,
Whimsy blooms in silent spots,
As joy finds life among the thoughts.

Curiosities Under the Stars

Underneath the twinkling lights,
Dancing dreams take playful flights,
Fluffy clouds make silly jokes,
As the sky giggles and pokes.

Stars put on their brightest ties,
Comets race and wave goodbyes,
A cat on a cloud plays chess,
While frogs in tuxes jest and jest.

Mice with capes on adventures roam,
Searching for their cosmic home,
The moon rolls his eyes at the fuss,
As laughter fills the stardust bus.

Curious hearts explore the night,
Finding wonder, pure delight,
With each shine and every glance,
The universe invites to dance.

Chirps of the Unseen

In gardens where the shadows play,
A cricket sings both night and day.
His tune is sweet, yet quite absurd,
He hums of things you've never heard.

A squirrel on a branch does dance,
Wearing not a single pants.
He leaps and twirls, what a fine show,
While vowing never to eat low.

The moon rolls in with silver glee,
Winking secrets, can you see?
It whispers tales of cats and mice,
And every trouble seems quite nice.

So gather ye the birds and bees,
Embrace the stumbles, quirks, and wheeze.
For in this jest, sweet moments gleam,
A world alive, a silly dream.

The Laughing Philosopher

With furrowed brow and twinkling eyes,
He ponders truths that banish lies.
"What if the sky is just a hat?"
He muses deep, sittin' with a cat.

The tea he sips is steeped in cheer,
He claims it cures all doubt and fear.
He laughs aloud at woes and strife,
And plays the trumpet, just for life!

"Is that a fish or just a shoe?"
He asks the crowd, who laugh anew.
With every thought, absurd and bold,
He weaves a tapestry of gold.

In every sneeze and crazy quirk,
He finds the joy, the fun, the work.
For wisdom's just a jester's grin,
And laughter hides the truth within.

Curiosities of the Ordinary

In a world where socks go free,
Why do they vanish? We can't see.
The toaster pops like it's in a race,
While crumbs conspire in secret space.

Jars of jelly dance at night,
Wiggling to tunes of pure delight.
The fridge hums jokes, cracked and old,
While all the leftovers slowly mold.

A cat that thinks it's a tiny king,
Wields its tail like a regal thing.
But where's the throne? Oh, next to the bed,
Amongst the socks and dreams we've shed.

When rain drops down with a silly song,
Puddles form, and we bounce along.
With whispers of joy in drops that jest,
We search for the quirks that life's expressed.

When Shadows Begin to Smile

At dusk, the shadows start to play,
They wear bright hats, oh what a display!
A tree whispers secrets like a big old pro,
While squirrels throw acorns like they're on show.

Moonbeams tickle the sleepy streets,
While night-time creatures shuffle their feet.
Do they have meetings to trade their tales?
Or swap their dreams like adventurous whales?

A shadowed cat, with mischievous flair,
Sips from the puddles, without a care.
Every nudge of the wind, a giggly ghost,
In the giggle of darkness, they seem to boast.

As stars wink down with a twinkling joke,
A frog croaks loudly in quirky cloak.
The night laughs softly, a jester divine,
In a world where shadows begin to shine.

An Odyssey Through the Unexpected

With coffee spills and scribbled notes,
We sail our boats made of paper coats.
A cat that winks, a fish that flies,
In dreams, we dance beneath the skies.

The fridge hums tunes of lost ballet,
While spoons conspire in a silly array.
Oh, where's my shoe? It vanished in night,
In a tale of socks and pure delight.

An apple rolls like a runaway king,
As laughter bubbles from the strangest spring.
Each twist and turn, we find surprise,
With questions that help us think and rise.

Through hallways lined with tales untold,
We stumble upon magic, bright and bold.
A quest for joy in mischief's hold,
Unlocks the heart, and stories unfold.

The Kaleidoscope of Existence

Colors swirl in a blender's dance,
Where ordinary things take a second chance.
A toast to crumbs that laugh at fate,
In the shuffle of socks, it truly is great.

The sun grins like a playful child,
While clouds giggle, whimsical and wild.
Each moment spins in a curious hue,
As we sip from cups brimming with goo.

Pancakes flipping with syncopated flair,
Whispering secrets in the morning air.
Tickling noses of morning's light,
Each day begins with a playful bite.

Mirrors chuckle, reflecting the jest,
As we ponder our quests with every quest.
In this kaleidoscope where we twirl and glide,
The ordinary shines, like a joyful ride.

The Puzzles We Dance Around

In a room full of socks, one goes astray,
The pair is confused, hip-hip-hooray!
Do buttons have dreams of a cozy night?
Or is it just seams that decide what's right?

The clock ticks backward, a songbirds fly,
We laugh at the fridge when it lets out a sigh.
Do shadows have secrets they whisper and share?
Or just plot their escape from the world's crazy flair?

Bananas on roller skates, what a sight!
They slip and they slide in a dance of delight.
The cheese wheels are grinning, what are they about?
Is it just the joy of living without a doubt?

In a world that's a puzzle, we spin and twirl,
Chasing our tails in a merry swirl.
With each piece we find, we chuckle aloud,
For in this mad game, we're a zany crowd.

Grins in the Shadows

Beneath the moonlight, a shadow may grin,
As it dances like no one, with cheer from within.
Do pencils confide when they lose their point?
Or do secrets reside in an empty joint?

In corners of rooms where the dust bunnies dwell,
They giggle away, oh, what stories they tell!
Are forks in a fight with spoons on a quest?
Or jesters in chaos, at their very best?

With laughter like bubbles, we rise and we fall,
Is that a door creaking, or a ghost at the hall?
What mischief awakes when the sun goes to sleep?
Do shadows hold jokes that they carefully keep?

In every dark space, an echo of glee,
As we skip through the twilight, wild and free.
Embracing the odd in the paths that we roam,
For joy's a reflection—we feel it at home.

Questions that Bloom

What if the flowers could giggle and sway,
Would daisies tell secrets to roses in May?
Do the clouds ever ponder just where they will roam?
Or are they content with the sky as their home?

When vegetables whisper, do we ever attend?
Or ignore all their jokes till the harvest's end?
Is a potato a friend or just part of the meal?
In gardens of wonder, how strange they appeal!

In fields of confusion, the butterflies tease,
As we chase after thoughts carried on the breeze.
What weight do we carry in bags of old dreams?
Are they truly as heavy as sunlight it seems?

With petals unfurling and laughter in air,
We question the answers, for life isn't fair.
Still, in every odd moment, with joy we consume,
In the fabric of blooming, let's dance and resume.

Quirks of Existence

Worms in a tangle, they swing and they sway,
In conversations of soil, they dance all day.
How long can a shelf hold a collection of spice?
Is life just a recipe, served up with ice?

At breakfast, the toast does a wobbly stand,
While pancakes flip high with a flick of the hand.
Do mirrors converse with reflections in show?
Or do they just sit back and enjoy the flow?

In every odd moment that glimmers and shines,
There's giggles in raindrops, in whimsical lines.
What notes do the clouds pass when thunder strikes fast?
Are they sharing some humor from days that have passed?

As quirks weave a tapestry vibrant and bright,
We relish each laugh that ignites the night.
In the absurd dance of this curious spin,
We find joy in the quirk of the world that we're in.

Reflections on a Broken Mirror

In every crack, a secret hides,
Reflecting faces, joy collides.
A wink, a frown, a silly dance,
Each shard, a chance for a second glance.

What's this face with a silly grin?
Is it me or just a twin?
With every joke, the glass will bend,
What madness will the mirror send?

The wrinkles tell of laughter's lore,
A thousand giggles from before.
In fractured truth, we play the part,
Of jesters with a knowing heart.

So raise a toast to cracks that gleam,
And silly thoughts that fuel our dream.
For in this chaos, oh so bright,
We find the charm in fractured light.

Tickles of the Twilight

When day turns to blush, the world takes flight,
The sky, a canvas of deepening night.
With fireflies dancing, oh what a sight,
They giggle and twirl, bringing pure delight.

The stars play peek-a-boo, quite the jest,
Winking like friends in a cosmic fest.
A clumsy moon trips over the clouds,
Launching laughter above the crowds.

In the hush of dark, the whispers play,
Chasing shadows that come out to sway.
What tales do they tell as they prance around?
Of dreams on the ground and giggles unbound?

So let's gather 'round, as twilight sings,
And catch the joy that evening brings.
With tickles and chuckles in soft twilight,
We'll dance in the dark, till morning's light.

Contradictions of a Grinning Soul

With every smile, a question looms,
Like jester's bells in crowded rooms.
Why so happy when chaos reigns?
What sense is found in twisted chains?

A heart that chuckles at burning woes,
Spinning tales where humor flows.
In every gaffe, a pearl appears,
Bound with laughter, wrapped in cheers.

What's hidden under a porcelain mask?
Is joy a game, or a foolish task?
With twinkly eyes and mischief's brew,
We dance on absurdities old and new.

So here's to the soul that laughs at fate,
With jokes as the only way to relate.
In the clamor of life's merry dance,
We find our peace in this playful chance.

Anecdotes from the Upside Down

In a world where ceilings kiss the ground,
And dogs wear hats, so profound.
The trees hum tunes, spinning tales,
While squirrels plot silly, grand-scale fails.

A cat on a skateboard, oh what a sight,
Belly flops win in a pillow fight.
Banana peels underfoot, watch your step,
Laughter lurking where giggles crept.

What wisdom from oddities sprout?
In the zany chaos, we laugh it out.
Wiggly chairs and wobbly stairs,
Tickling notions that float through the air.

So tip your hat to the upside-down,
Where joy is worn like a vibrant crown.
In tales of whimsy, we'll delight and spin,
For it's here in the quirky, we truly win.

Snickers Beneath the Surface

Beneath the quirk of every grin,
Lies a riddle wrapped in skin.
Why do ducks wear yellow shoes?
Is it fashion or just to amuse?

In the corner, a cat wearing a hat,
Looks quite wise, but what's up with that?
Can a dog play chess or just pretend?
With a wag of the tail, he'll always blend.

A juggler drops a spoon, how absurd!
Did he plan it, or is it unheard?
As giggles chase the falling pie,
"You missed it!" is the most common cry.

Laughter echoes off the walls,
Tickles the brain, as reason stalls.
In every chuckle, a plot unfurls,
To turn the mundane into pearls.

Ponderings of a Playful Mind

Why do socks always go astray?
Do they conspire to fray the day?
Do pancakes dream of syrup streams?
Or is it just the toast that beams?

A turtle racing to the moon,
Calls out, "I'll be back real soon!"
While fish in space plot their next dive,
As aliens check their sailor jive.

Chasing shadows with a broom,
"Can they dance?" echoes in the room.
Why do chairs make silly faces?
In the dark, they find their places.

Cereal talks on Tuesday morn,
While yarn-ball cats are somewhat worn.
Perhaps tomorrow, they might just sing,
As we unravel each little thing.

The Semantics of Surprise

A pickle wearing sunglasses cool,
Shouts, "Pick me!" at the swimming pool.
Balloons debate their colors bright,
"Is being orange wrong or right?"

What's the secret to a good balloon?
To float or not? That is the tune.
A fish with legs hops on the floor,
Says, "What's freedom if I can't explore?"

Underneath the table, there's a cat,
Baking plans with a furry brat.
As giggles spill into the air,
Do we find logic hiding there?

With a twist of fate, an umbrella spins,
Unraveling mysteries of tiny sins.
Was it real or just a game?
As the world stirs, nothing's the same.

Chuckles in the Chaos

In the midst of a swirling mess,
A talking broom will surely bless.
Do pigeons gossip on their coos?
What's the latest on the morning news?

A hamster in a tiny car,
Claims he'll drive us near and far.
The lamp stands tall, tips its shade,
As shadows dance, a charade is made.

Chocolate rivers flow with glee,
Can I take a swim and maybe see?
The spoons rejoice in midnight chats,
While cookies dream of conquering bats.

With each chuckle, the winds will howl,
As giggles spread, it's chaos we'll bow.
In this whirl, embrace the jest,
For a quirky tale is simply the best.

Searching for the Simple Truth

A squirrel wearing socks found a nut,
It pondered the meaning of a hungry gut.
A wise old owl hooted with glee,
"Why ponder the nut? Just climb a tree!"

The clouds overhead looked quite bemused,
As ants in a parade felt quite confused.
"What is the purpose?" they marched and marched,
While a passing snail said, "I'm just starched!"

The sun winked down, as if to tease,
"Why look for answers in the buzzing bees?"
The flowers giggled, swaying side to side,
And the breeze whispered secrets like it tried to hide.

So let the questions flutter and fly,
For the truth's just a glance, like a butterfly.
Chase it and chase it, but know the refrain:
It's really just fun, like a circus train!

Notes from a Peculiar Hour

The clock struck thirteen, a cat wore a hat,
While a jellybean danced with a curious rat.
A blender proclaimed, "I'll mix up your dreams!"
As everyone shrugged and sipped on whipped creams.

A fish on a bicycle swam through the park,
While pigeons in tuxedos remarked with a squawk.
"Is this all crazy?" asked a dainty leaf,
But laughter erupted in a riotous brief.

A toaster was dating an old rusty pan,
They whispered sweet nothings, a fantastic plan.
A cupcake was pondered, but held on tight:
"Why chase tomorrow when we have tonight?"

Notes scribbled in crayons adorned the sky,
As stars giggled softly, flying bye-bye.
The peculiar hour just giggled in shine,
Eat cake, take a nap, and drink fizzy brine!

Tales of the Unexplained

A chap lost his shoelace to a rogue little shoe,
A duck quacked inquiries no one ever knew.
The jelly on the shelf made a daring escape,
Wiggling with plans to reshape the landscape.

A talking toaster dreamed of toasted bread bliss,
While a pickle in a jar complained about this.
"What's in a tale?" asked a bright yellow cuke,
"Just dreams of a world where no one's a fluke!"

The stars in their formation seemed to conspire,
As a spoon asked a fork, "What's your greatest desire?"
They laugh at the stories we spin every night,
Like wishes on cupcakes that float out of sight.

So gather your fables, your giggles, your fright,
For mysteries twirl like a kite in the light.
In a world that's so strange, let's celebrate glee,
And dance with the shadows, just you and me!

Whims of the Wandering Soul

A dandelion wished to float far away,
While a confused pinecone rolled into play.
"What's it like out there?" asked a curious snail,
"With cabinets singing and ships made of kale?"

A pancake serenaded the grapefruit one morn,
While a sad old pancake felt utterly torn.
"What's wrong with my flip?" it sighed with regret,
While a squirrel nearby just gambled with debt.

The whispers of wind told stories of old,
Of clouds made of cotton and stars crafted gold.
As moons juggled oranges in the midnight air,
A merry raccoon proclaimed, "Let's not be bare!"

So we wander and wonder with whimsy in place,
In a world painted bright, with laughter and grace.
To question the reasons and chase every fun,
Is to live with a smile, like a melody spun!

The Jester's Riddle

Why did the chicken cross the room?
To find a hat and escape the gloom.
A pickle danced on the kitchen floor,
And laughed at the cat who wanted more.

A shoe found a sock, they twirled with glee,
An old spoon whispered, "Come dance with me!"
The walls started giggling, a ticklish tease,
While the fridge hummed a tune that would please.

A tumbleweed rolled through a toaster's snare,
As a clock ticked backward, unaware.
The windows were cracked with smiles so bright,
In the realm of nonsense, it's always night.

So raise a toast to this comical feat,
To riddles and jesters, life's playful beat.
For in every strange chuckle, we find a spark,
That lights up our days, even in the dark.

Echoes of the Mundane

In a land where socks go to disappear,
A spoon had a dream to become a seer.
The dust bunnies plotted a theatrical play,
While the vacuum cleaner just wanted to sway.

A coffee mug said, "I'm feeling quite grand,"
As it brewed up ideas no one could stand.
The remote control plotted its great escape,
Into the couch where all lost treasures drape.

Tiny voices in the teacups would sneer,
"Your butter's too soft, let's make it career!"
They argued for hours, what a delicious fight,
In the echoes of chaos, all felt so right.

When the kettle whistled, it sang a duet,
With the toaster's pop song, no one could regret.
In shadows of cabinets, joy leaves its trace,
Smiling in bits of the mundane's embrace.

Smiles in Unlikely Places

A squirrel wore glasses, reading a book,
While ants held a meeting, planning to cook.
The banana peel plotted a grand slip,
As bubbles in soda prepared for a trip.

The garden gnome winked with an upturned thumb,
While the flowers debated who'd dance and hum.
A giggle erupted from the old rusty swing,
As laughter erupted, a marvellous thing.

Inside the shoe, where lost coins reside,
A penny recounted its long, wild ride.
With every odd moment, joy takes its chance,
In peculiar corners, the funny ones dance.

So cherish the quirks, the mishaps and fumbles,
For within these small wonders, the spirit stumbles.
Each smile brings color, a whimsical trace,
In the most unlikely, we find our embrace.

Musings of a Wandering Heart

A rogue balloon floated high in the sky,
It wondered aloud why time passes by.
A goldfish inquiring on tales from the shore,
While a curious cactus dreamed of galore.

The mango had plans to dance with the peach,
As moonlight waltzed with a soft, gentle breach.
They giggled at clouds, fluffy and immense,
Creating an opera, all in pretense.

Each daisy tried hard to offer advice,
To the wandering heart, just rolling the dice.
With hope in each petal that whispered so sweet,
"Embrace every moment, let laughter repeat."

So here's to the journey, the odd and the strange,
Where smiles take shape and thoughts gently change.
In musings of wonder, our spirits take flight,
Finding joy in the echoes of day and night.

www.ingramcontent.com/pod-product-compliance
Lightning Source LLC
Chambersburg PA
CBHW051638160426
43209CB00004B/694